May all yo
pleasures be filled
peace and joy —
        Keep paddlin' on—
            May De

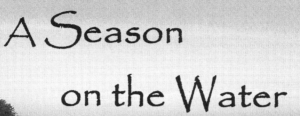

A Season

on the Water

Reflections
from the Red Kayak

by
MARY ANNE SMRZ

An NBCS, Inc. Production

Email: info@redkayakinstitute.org
Website: www.redkayakinstitute.org

A Season on the Water: Reflections from the Red Kayak
Second Edition
Copyright © 2012 Mary Anne Smrz

Published in the United States by Pearl Editions, LLC.

Cover and book design and layout by Josette Songco.
Photographs by Mary Anne Smrz, unless otherwise noted.
Printed in the United States of America.

ISBN **978-1-7325578-0-2**

The purpose of this book is to inspire and comfort. The information is designed to acquaint individuals with the process of journaling as a way to gain insight. Neither the author nor the publisher is engaged in rendering medical or counseling advice. If such advice is required, the services of a qualified medical professional should be sought. The author and publisher shall not be held liable or responsible to any person or entity with respect to any loss or damage caused or alleged to be caused, directly or indirectly by the information contained in this publication.

1. Diaries Authorship. 2. Journals Authorship. 3. Journal writing. 4. Kayaking 5. Nature journaling 6. Mind-body connections

To Joan Anderson,
as unfinished as the
shoreline along the beach

Acknowledgements

"We all have a story to tell whether we publish it
or keep it just for ourselves or family.
Allow yourself to be heard."

~Anonymous

There are so many people to acknowledge in this second in a series of *Reflections from the Red Kayak* that I struggle with where to begin. Since the writing of the first book, *Thoughts on Life*, I am continually amazed at how the sharing of my thoughts has touched so many people. I am humbled by the number of people who reached back to me with their thoughts and comments.

I am deeply grateful to so many of you who purchased the initial book and shared it with family and friends. Your support of my journey and my message is an incredible source of ongoing inspiration. You know who you are!

To all my paddling buddies this season, your stories echo throughout these pages. My "season on the water" is complete with the sharing of our time and our selves.

From the bottom of my heart thank you to my dear friend Jackie Messner in Wisconsin. You were the first one to purchase a book from me, and that surprising, initial affirmation means so much. I will always keep that first $20 bill as a reminder of how deeply your encouragement touches me and how rich our friendship is becoming.

To my business partner, Jason Dobrzynski, for all the times you take care of things at the office so that I can get away to paddle and write, you are truly a blessing in my life. This second writing could not have been possible without your support and encouragement.

I thank Sister Lois Bromark, "Str," my high school religion teacher, who I reconnected with through Jan Malloy's work at Mother McAuley High School, and Sister Dorothy Lucille, "Dottie Lou," my high school principal. In your support of my first book, you reconnect me with my carefree, high school years and a thread that brings so much of my life full circle.

To my cherished friends Sallie and Ken King, for taking time out of your own lives to stay with my yellow lab, Bayfield, while I head to Sedona and other places to visit and paddle. I could not do this without you staying at my home and caring for Bayfield.

A special note of gratitude to Danny Kuklinski. Our insightful conversations, your beautiful letter about my book and your gift of the fabulous dragonfly photo are inspiring and touching. I look forward to the creativity that continues to emerge from your young spirit.

To my late friend, Kathy MacNeil, who said, "It tastes like another," anytime she enjoyed something so much and wanted more. The echo of your voice provided a prodding whisper for this book, this "another."

A note of deep appreciation to Sue Morris, for your friendship and for sharing my first book with our friend, Margie. The tender story of how the book uplifted her during the unrelenting challenges of chemotherapy touched a chord deep within me and kept me writing with an inner passion I cannot explain. Thank you for always keeping me tethered to my beloved northwoods.

Many thanks to Betsy Oliver and Kathy Mekley, for the cute little canoeing verse that you transformed into a kayaking poem. "Love many, watch your back, and always paddle your own kayak." I love it! That little gift of inspiration means so much. To Abby Malloy, for coming to stay with Bayfield while I took my final, "Season on the Water" trip to Cape Cod, you have no idea how much this meant to me. You are treasured family and a wonderful friend who played an important role in the completion of this book.

Special thanks to Art Durham, for getting my website up and running this year. I am clueless as to how that all happens and your guidance and willingness to continually keep me on task is invaluable.

As I continue to "paddle on," I am deeply grateful to Ann Moss for the new logo design. Your creativity never ceases to amaze me and how fitting that we came to the final design at our beloved "Ashram." Thank you for the wonderful stamp you have put on this project.

A sincere note of thanks to Lucas Durham, for your expert photographic enhancements and the beautiful shell composition. It means so much to have your ever-emerging artistry resonate throughout these pages.

To Josette Songco, for our joyful brainstorming sessions, your exquisite design of this book and your imaginative ideas. Your endearing friendship and willingness to paddle this journey of life with me provide sustenance for my soul.

As always, heartfelt gratitude to Georgiann Baldino, my editor, publisher and dear friend. I deeply appreciate you sifting through every draft and fussing over my grammar. Your clear and steady guidance provides the framework for this book, and our ever-deepening friendship means the world to me.

Whenever I explore or expand my creativity, I must thank my mom. Your encouragement of my talents from early on provides an ongoing source of motivation for me and for that, and you, I am grateful.

To Bayfield, my ever-present and loyal companion. I treasure having you nearby on your dog pillow while I write, and I love our fun-filled and adventurous Wisconsin odysseys. Your continual "puppy" antics bring joy to my soul. You are the true essence of the saying by Collette, "Our perfect companions never have fewer than four feet."

And finally, to the late "Mary" Jan Malloy, my paddling partner. Your message to me, "I hope it goes real well for you," makes me smile and helps me to remember that our departed loved ones are always nearby. Your memory, your spirit and your kayak journey with me throughout this "season on the water."

Paddlin'

MARY ANNE SMRZ
MARCH, 2012

Table of Contents

Be Generative

PROLOGUE

Be Generative

"When through one woman
a little more love and goodness,
a little more light and truth come into the world –
then that woman's life has had meaning."

-Anonymous

PROLOGUE

My yellow Labrador Retriever Bayfield and I are on one of our Wisconsin odysseys this long September weekend. I am in a pensive, contemplative mood on this gray, rainy day. The dull, overcast sky and gentle rain have a way of quieting me down, as though the heavens are saying, "just rest." A good day to hunker in as I begin this book.

I pour myself a cup of my favorite Organic Wilderness Retreat coffee, light my balsam fir candle and head to the loft to write. I open the shades to the expanse of the lake, and let the soft light stream in. While my computer boots up, I sit in a wooden rocker my aunt Jean gave me many years ago at a time of unsettling transition in my life. She was a great lady, stately I would say. I spent many of my early years at the corner grocery store she owned with my uncle Hank, located across the street from a playground. Who could have crafted a more blissful childhood than that? A neighborhood grocery store complete with the best selection of candy and ice cream and a playground where my spirit could run free. A loving extended family complete with my two cousins,

Steve and Gary, who were like older brothers to me. I think about my aunt Jean now and one of the great lessons I learned from her. She always trusted me and in doing so, taught me how to trust others. I am grateful for her positive influence in my life.

I sit at my computer and momentarily reflect back to the publishing of *Reflections from the Red Kayak: Thoughts on Life* in 2010. By the encouraging response of my readers, I am inspired to continue my writing. The book touches people in many unexpected ways and helps others "paddle on" their own journeys. It is from this humble place of sharing that I write this next book.

The story really begins in April of 2010. I attended one of Joan Anderson's "Weekend to Change Your Life" retreats on Whidbey Island off the coast of Washington State. Joan is an internationally renowned author and I had read all of her books. Her messages and insights totally resonated with me.

I was at a time of significant 'change thrust upon me', as Joan would say, having suffered through three significant losses in my life in a very short period of time. My life was turned upside down and in working through the circular, unpredictable cycles of grief, I was exhausted. I longed to retreat. I needed a place unfamiliar, a place with no memories and no agenda. I ached for an open space to simply "be," and take a small step for myself to begin the process of rearranging the scattered puzzle pieces of my life. At the retreat, I promised myself to just stay open to the experience.

Among all the majesty of the landscape of Whidbey, the simple gnarly tree pictured at the opening of this prologue captured me. Amidst all its imperfections, beautiful flowers blossomed on its twisted branches. In this tree I saw a true snapshot of my life. It helped me realize that within the tangled knots of my sorrow and confusion, healing and peacefulness would find their place.

I fell in love with the beauty and grandeur of the Pacific Northwest and returned home with a tiny glimpse of my new self and a renewed sense of purpose. From this small space of inner renovation I wrote *Reflections from the Red Kayak: Thoughts on Life* and sent Joan a copy for Christmas that year.

Fast forward one year later to April, 2011, and Joan is coming to Rockford, Illinois, as the keynote speaker at the spring luncheon for the non-profit organization, Womanspace. I was excited to go with five of my friends to see Joan again and to hear her speak. I was in need of her refreshing insight and empowering words, her sense of seeking and her recognition of our unfinished journeys. Having been in contact with Joan periodically throughout the year, I hoped to connect with her for breakfast or dinner while she was in town. I could not have imagined what transpired next.

We emailed each other prior to her coming and she promised to call me. Two days before the Saturday luncheon, her first call to me from Logan Airport went to voice mail, and you can imagine my utter disappointment. She promised to call again and I never let my cell phone out of my possession until we connected the next day.

Talking to her again was empowering in and of itself. We settled on dinner plans for Sunday evening before she headed back home to Cape Cod. I was thrilled and excited to have a chance to reconnect on a personal level with Joan. What happened next was even more astonishing.

Before we hung up, Joan asked me if I had a copy of my book. I said I did and she asked me to bring it to the luncheon.

I replied, "Why?" and she answered that she often speaks of retreaters during her keynotes and wanted to mention me and my book. Again, I said, "Why?" feeling perplexed.

She responded, "Because when I met you at Whidbey you were in a deep hole, and with the writing of your book you have shared yourself and are working your way through your grief. It is a great story."

Astounded, I said OK. I couldnt have imagined a greater honor. What came next was even more amazing.

"By the way, do you have a lot of books?" she asked.

At this point I must stop and say I was taken aback by serendipity. I had run out of the first printing of books and just ordered another, scheduled to be ready the following week. About an hour before this conversation with Joan, the printer called to say my books were finished early and I could pick them up anytime.

Smiling I replied, "Yes, as a matter of fact, I have more books."

"Well bring a box," she directed me.

Again I said, "Why?"

"Because I'm going to set you up at the table next to me. You and me, we'll be signing books together."

Now I am completely astonished. I could only say OK again, and I hung up the phone trying to fully absorb the incredible conversation that had just transpired.

Can you even imagine the honor and privilege it was for me, an unknown author with my first publication, signing books beside an internationally renowned author of five books and someone who I have admired and respected for over ten years? She broke protocol and stepped out of her own comfort zone to include me in her sacred space. This shared experience was incredible.

In addition to the book signing with Joan, one of the best things about the luncheon was sharing the day with my special, dear friends – Janie Ford, Mary Lavine, Deb Maschmeier, Ann Moss and Josette Songco. It was a magical day and our table was the luckiest one at the luncheon.

Joan was gracious to offer each of her five books as raffle prizes. As the drawing for the winners began, we sat in anticipation. The first winner was called, someone at another table. The second winning pick was my friend, Deb. We eagerly applauded and had the collective feeling that something special was unfolding. Then my name was selected and our enthusiasm heightened. I went to the podium and Joan asked me, 'Which of my books don't you have?"

"I have all of them," I replied and suggested she pick another name. The next winner? Josette Songco! The exuberance at our table went to a higher level.

The selection of the raffle gifts and silent auction prizes continued until the highly coveted grand prize, a trip for eight to Sedona, Arizona. The entire luncheon of 325 women waited in high anticipation of the winner and when the name was drawn – Mary Lavine! We could not contain ourselves! We were wild with the incredible energy of this day and we were going to Sedona!

Joan's affirmation of me and the unbounded energy of that day carried me through the completion of this book. Often when I was stuck with my writing, I opened one of Joan's books and read a few chapters. That process helped to restore the cadence and tone of my writing. And I would think of that incredible day.

Like putting my kayak in the water and pushing off from shore, I have been "launched," as Joan later told me. Where the journey takes me now is unknown, but my heart remains open to the possibilities, to the magical moments yet to come.

When I attended the retreat at Whidbey, I felt that I was in ebb tide. Joan describes it in *A Year by the Sea* as "the water is not going anywhere, neither coming in or going out, ebb tide, I suppose-the sea at a standstill as am I."I felt completely like that. My life was at a standstill. I just had to be content to be in my own ebb tide. Patience is not one of my strong suits, but I had neither the energy nor the enthusiasm to try to move in any direction.

Now, almost two years later, I feel as though I am slowly moving forward, maybe not high tide, but certainly no longer in ebb tide. I continue to be willing to stay open to the new. I have only decided one thing, as

Joan says, "to entertain change rather than stay stuck in the familiar."

I admire Joan's courage in stepping away for her year by the sea. Courage comes from the Latin word *corage*, which means 'from the heart.' I believe that when you are true to yourself and follow your heart, whatever you do will be right not only for you, but for those around you. Because of her "corage" Joan helps so many women acknowledge and appreciate their unfinished selves. I am honored and grateful to be one of those women.

My first book, *Reflections from the Red Kayak: Thoughts on Life* has taken on a life of its own. It impacts people differently and its message unfolds in its own way. In the continuation of this journey, I am only a conduit for the thoughts and insights that come from my time on the water. "Paddle on" has become the mantra now for me and so many of my readers.

I go back to Joan's words, "Be generative." Pass along what you know. It comes from her friendship with Joan Erikson, who was married to the famous psychoanalyst Erik Erikson. Joan Erikson said, and I quote from Anderson's book *The Second Journey*, "The most important thing is to share what you know. Be generative. Pass it on. That is what makes all the difference."

It is in this spirit of "being generative" that I embark on the completion of this second book, *A Season on the Water: Reflections from the Red Kayak*. It is for her inspiration and affirmation, that I dedicate this book to Joan, my mentor and friend.

As I always close each section with questions for you to ponder, I leave you with these thoughts from Joan's book, *A Weekend to Change your Life:*

"To let myself be carried, to yield to unseen currents and be made to drift, is my primary challenge now."

"What do you get when you dare to see all of your choices and follow out the ones that speak to you alone? "

"What happens when you stand up for yourself and decide to live boldly?"

"What can you do in your own life to be generative?"

"How can you pass along what you know and leave" your eternal mark?

Photo by Josette Songco

"You cannot step into
the same river twice.
Each time is different
and so are you."
- Heraclitus

Change

WELCOME SPRING

Change

"Even the seasons form a great circle
in their changing,
and always come back again
to where they were."
-Black Elk

WELCOME SPRING

I took a few days off this April weekend to retreat and relax at my lake house in central Wisconsin. In addition to much needed rest, it was my intention to begin some outdoor spring projects, like mulching the flower beds and cleaning up the yard from winter's debris.

Mother Nature, however, had other plans. A spring snowstorm blanketed Wisconsin the day before and as I drove the country roads north, glistening hoarfrost on the trees and 3 inches of sparkling snow welcomed me. Winter's grasp on the Midwest continued. On my ride, I called my aunt Stef. She and I shared many drives through Wisconsin together, filled with great conversation, laughter and the sharing of non-stop snacks. It is our ritual to always connect with each other each time I head north.

I called my mom when I arrived to give her the snow report. She loves the weather as I do and she said, "Welcome spring!" Indeed.

I had also intended to get my kayak on the water for the first highly anticipated paddle of the season, which is always a treasured delight. After I unpacked, took my yellow lab, Bayfield for a hike in the snow and had a quick lunch, a light snow began to fall. I looked out at the water. The water looked back at me. I smiled. According to the calendar, spring officially arrived almost a month ago.

"Should I?" I asked myself.

Why not,"I said to Bayfield, who was watching my every move.

Some things just cant wait and when Mother Nature gives you an unexpected gift, I believe you must seize the moment and open the package.

I hauled out my favorite winter maroon and white UMass hat with a white tassel on top, my L.L. Bean® Vortex paddling gloves and my winter jacket. I donned 2 layers of pants and put on my wool socks and boots. I looked like Nanook of the North'ready to go snowshoeing, not kayaking. I had never paddled with so much clothing on before and never paddled when it was snowing. The adventure was upon me.

Sliding my kayak down to the water in the freshly fallen snow was a fun, new experience for both me and my little red vessel. It is my tradition to always take my first kayak, the red one my friends gave me for my birthday 16 years ago, on the inaugural ride of the season. Like two old friends we prepare to hit the water together sharing the sacred moment. The temperature was 35°; the winds were WNW at 7 m.p.h. making it feel like a balmy 29°. Ideal conditions for a spring paddle, I told myself and smiled. Time to launch!

The first outing of the new season is always a special one for me. All the reasons why I love to kayak come rushing forth in that first exhilarating instant of pushing off from shore and dipping my paddle in the water. Paddling solo, I keep close to the shore. After all, the ice out has just occurred. Ice out is when the winter tundra of ice on the lake reverts back to water. A frosty dip in the frigid lake is definitely not on my itinerary today!

Paddling with the blowing snow in my face and seeing the snow on shore, I thought about how we must always adapt. Mother Nature, in all her beauty and glory, often conforms to us, and we must change with her.

Just as this season is slowly changing from winter to spring, our lives are continually changing. Most days, the changes are fairly subtle, unrecognizable almost. Other days, more significant occurrences bring forth greater adversity. By and large as humans, we resist change. We avoid it like the plague. Like paddling upstream, we fight it every stroke of the way. Why is that?

Change renders something new. Sometimes the change is welcome. We joyfully go forward, anticipating the refreshingly unfamiliar shift in our lives. Other times change is thrust upon us, and we find ourselves in unwanted and unexpected circumstances. In either case, havent we learned from so many previous transitions that ultimately change is good? And haven't we gained the understanding that the transformation was necessary to our growth, whether it was something we wanted or not? The one thing I know for sure is that without change, we live the same day over and over again.

I think, like this time of year on the water, that the hardest part of any transition is the middle. The time when I am no longer in the old place but not yet in the new. The time when the way is unclear and the next step is uncertain, yet there is no going back. Just like this seasonal shift, no longer really winter but not yet spring.

Paddling on, I heard the nuthatch chirping and the cardinals singing their mating calls, trying to egg spring on. The snow falling from the pine trees was pelting the water in chunks and it was amazing to observe how the snow instantly turned into water. On a smaller scale, it reminded me of kayaking in front of Columbia Glacier in Alaska six years ago and witnessing the ice calving. Water is always transforming itself, I thought, and we are, too. Every day our bodies are changing, our thoughts are different and our paths shift ever so slightly.

The hour long paddle was refreshing and invigorating. Arriving home, I quickly changed into some fresh warm clothes. I was going to put on a dry sweatshirt; and then changed my mind. I opened the bifold closet door of the bedroom my family still affectionately calls, "Dad's room," even though he's been gone almost three years. I donned his favorite black and white plaid flannel shirt that lovingly hangs there, letting the warmth of his memory surround me. As I buttoned the shirt, I looked down at the edge of the sleeve and noticed a splotch of paint, a reminder of the last time he was here in Wisconsin with me. We did a painting project together. Although my dad didn't like to paint he was always willing to put a brush in his hand with me. The sweet memory of that time made me smile and cry at the same time.

Wearing his shirt I again thought about that word "change" and aren't we always adapting to the continual shifts in our lives? Whether good or bad, happy or sad, gain or loss, we have a choice about the changes we experience. We can either resist or we can adapt.

I am learning that it is much easier to adapt, to go with the flow and allow the changes to provide the current to take me to the next place. My friend Ann Moss always reminds me to remember what my life was five years ago, acknowledge where it is today and imagine where it will be five years from now. The only thing I know for certain is that it will be different; it will be changed.

I made myself a cup of hot chocolate to enjoy with a slice of my friend Mary Lavine's scrumptious homemade banana nut bread. I curled up on the futon with Bayfield, sat back and relished the freshness of the first paddle, now complete. Welcome spring!

Spring is the season of new beginnings. What changes are you adapting to and how have they impacted you?

Can you seamlessly incorporate those changes into your life, or is it going to take some time and energy?

Are you resisting or adapting?

Belief

WHAT A DIFFERENCE A DAY MAKES

Belief

> "We have always held to the hope,
> the belief, the conviction that
> there is a better life, a better world
> beyond the horizon."
> -Franklin D Roosevelt

WHAT A DIFFERENCE A DAY MAKES

The spring season in Wisconsin continued to adapt and change and I awoke the next day to very different weather. Yesterday's snowfall gave way to warmer temperatures and sunshine! Yes, sunshine! Here in the Midwest we have been beleaguered with so many cloudy days during this winter and early spring that the sun seems like a foreign object in the sky.

Another day for kayaking, I decided. I was greeted this day by two Common Loons on the water. They normally pass through central Wisconsin this time of year on their way to the northwoods. I just love loons! I was anxious to be outside and get on with the day.

I grabbed my walking stick and took Bayfield for our three mile shoreline hike -a real treat for both of us. Today's hike was all about the big birds - four immature Bald Eagles and a Great Blue Heron. One of the special things about this peaceful hiking trail is that in the silence, I can hear the sounds of the bird's wings flapping as they lift off before I see them. I feel as though I can take flight with them. We hiked to the edge of a waterside ridge and sat on a rock, soaking in the glory and warmth of the sun.

I checked the temperature when we returned. 45°, winds from the south at 6 m.p.h. making it feel like 42°. It is a much better day to paddle, even though a southerly wind created choppier conditions on the lake. "Carpe diem," I said to Bayfield. Time to get out on the water.

As I prepare to go kayaking, I think about how nature teaches me to believe. After the rain comes the rainbow. After a forest fire, new growth emerges. After yesterday's snowfall, a day graced with warmth and sunshine. In life too, we often find brighter days after a difficult period. True, things are different, but if we truly believe that change is for the better, then we allow sunlit rays of hope and new found joy to enter in.

I am learning to trust in the deep conviction that current cycles of my life will transition to the next, and I put my faith in a brighter tomorrow. Nature provides a sanctuary for us to garner these life lessons. I believe in the process of change and a positive outcome. Just like the seasonal shifts, each transition prepares the inner landscape for a more buoyant tomorrow.

My dear friend, Pearl Copp, a great pioneering woman of the northwoods, once called me an eternal optimist. What an endearing compliment from a woman I have admired for 46 years. She and her husband, Fred, own the resort we go to each summer. She lives her life from her own authenticity, surrounded by nature and in tune with the seasons. Pearl is a woman of strong faith and belief, and a positive influence in her own, quiet way.

Anyway, on to the water. No winter hat or jacket today, just my trusty Life is Good® kayaking hat and my windbreaker. Even though I still had a few layers of clothing on, this was a little more like it. I paddled along the shoreline that Bayfield and I had just hiked. Looking at our path from the water, I saw the light brown bushy tail of a coyote whisk by and further down I noticed the silhouette of a deer ambling through the woods. How could life be grander?

About two weeks ago, powerful winds in excess of 70 m.p.h. ripped through this area, and a tornado touched down two miles to the northeast. Piles of debris were hurled upon the rocky waterside – branches, tree trunks and entire trees were slammed into the water. I can only imagine the wild fury of waves on the lake, an unbridled expression of Mother Nature in one of her fiercest moods!

This scene reminded me of kayaking last year in Puget Sound on the retreat on Whidbey Island. I was honored to paddle tandem with Cathy Stollen, an experienced kayaker from the Jersey shore, and we kayaked the Sound in silence. What a conflicting statement – the "Sound" in "silence." A 5-hour stretch of complete silence was part of this phenomenal retreat experience.

Kayaking along that seashore, two things simultaneously came into view for me – a sandy stretch of beach with huge stacks of driftwood hurled onto its shore, and a Bald Eagle gracefully soaring overhead. I remember thinking about my life circumstances at that retreat. Change, like so many pieces of debris, had been heaved atop me. I was buried under a pile of transition I neither wanted nor welcomed, but had to accept. Then I looked up and realized what I really wanted was to take flight like that Bald Eagle. Tears streamed down my salty face as I realized the journey from shore to sky was a long one for me indeed. I was so broken.

Paddling now, I remembered a quote by E.D. Martin that said, "It is easier to believe than to doubt." After Whidbey, I believed my path would be smoother and my life brighter. I just didn't know how.

Now, one year later, as I recollected that special memory and took stock of where I am in life today, I joyfully realized that I felt more like the eagles Bayfield and I saw earlier than the storm strewn debris on the shore. I bowed my head, honored the moment and said a prayer of gratitude for the sunshine that has come into my life.

We know that the sun still shines, even on cloudy, dreary days. No matter what your day is today, do you believe you can bring some sunshine into your life?

How strong is your conviction for positive change?

What people, places or things always add a ray of sunshine for you? Today, seize them and shine!

Discovery
SHORELINE SLEUTHING

Discovery

"A traveler am I and a navigator,
and every day I discover
a new region within my soul."
-Kahlil Gibran

SHORELINE SLEUTHING

When I was a young girl, I loved to read the Nancy Drew books. Nancy Drew was a fictional young amateur detective created by Edward Stratemeyer. The books were ghostwritten by a number of authors and were published under the collective pseudonym Carolyn Keene. Nancy first appeared in 1930, and the books were extensively revised from 1959-1971. She is considered a cultural icon, and has been cited as a formative influence by a number of prominent women; from Supreme Court Justices Sandra Day OConnor and Sonia Sotomayor to Secretary of State Hillary Rodham Clinton and former First Lady Laura Bush.

I could hardly wait for each new edition and when it arrived, Id stay up half the night reading page after glorious page. Nancy Drew, being the daughter of a lawyer, was adept at solving mysteries, and every book brought a new challenge. Each suspenseful chapter ending was a page turner and I could hardly put the book down. At that time, books were also published about the Dana Girls and the Hardy Boys, but for me there was nothing like Nancy Drew.

The entire 51-book collection has been sitting on a shelf in my mom's basement all these years. Recently, I decided to re-read those books in sequence, hoping to recollect and garnish what I loved so dearly about Nancy Drew. Sometimes, we must journey back to our childhood. We revisit the things we loved that brought us to who we are today. I resolved to take this journey, to see if there are nuggets in those books that I have kept with me through the years. Hidden clues to remind me of my own truths.

I have just read the first two books, *The Secret of the Old Clock* and *The Hidden Staircase*. A book I received from my dear friends Nancy Cassell and Pat Stejskal called *The Nancy Drew Sleuth Book: Clues to Good Sleuthing*, provided handy tips for a good detective! What I rediscovered about Nancy is that she loves to go out sleuthing and longs for new adventure. I connected with that.

I, too, can't wait for my next undertaking and this morning's weather presents a perfect kayaking opportunity. The temperature is 53°, the sky is partly cloudy and the winds are a mere breeze from the east so the water is perfectly calm. I call this a banner morning!"After paddling last month in the snow, donned in layers of winter clothing, the conditions this May morning call for my Life is Good™ paddling shorts and a t-shirt. Paddling as it should be! Like Nancy Drew, I was anxious for my morning's adventure to begin to do some "shoreline sleuthing" of my own.

I love to paddle the shoreline to discover interesting treasures. Today I am looking for driftwood sticks, about four feet high with interesting characteristics and a good thickness about them. I recently invented my own hobby of making walking sticks from these shoreline gifts. They are quite deluxe if I say so myself – complete with an embedded compass and six, one-inch hash marks on the bottom to measure depths of water one might encounter while hiking.

While kayaking this morning, my mind drifted back to my younger days. At the same time I began reading Nancy Drew, my family took annual summer vacations to northern Wisconsin. Once during the week there, I would take the rowboat out and circumvent the shoreline of the lake, looking for interesting pieces of driftwood to bring home. I'd bleach them, sand and stain them on my dad's workbench in his garage. I'd create pieces you could hang or pieces for a shelf and still have some of those early creations.

Drifting back in my memory to that time in my life, I remembered a few things about myself that had gotten slightly buried over the years. I loved to be creative and make something out of nothing. I rediscovered how much I enjoyed working with wood and the feeling of satisfaction to complete a project. I think I always loved that part the best – bringing things to fruition. Projects like these were an intricate puzzle for me to solve, or like Nancy Drew, an intriguing mystery to unravel.

Today is a good day for gathering sticks. The calm water allows me to kayak close to the rocky shore without being battered about and I collect some real keepers. I get lost in the search, watching each new set of rocks with an eye toward an interesting stick. Soon, my kayak looks more like a barge as I pile stick after stick on my front bow and hatch. Before I know it, two hours have passed and I have a collection of 12 sticks which will eventually be transformed into walking sticks. I've also picked up a few other interesting pieces of driftwood which I carefully balance on the hatch behind me. Now I am really on a discovery mission!

Sometimes, when I am paddling with my friend, Mary Lavine, we go sleuthing together, calling it our "service project." I'm really not sure why we call it that, but we take my other smaller kayak, tie it to the back of hers, and fill it with a collection of interesting things we gather from the shore. Like the sea shells Anne Morrow Lindbergh wrote about in *Gift from the Sea,* we collect our own special "gifts from the lake." Mary would be amazed at my collection today.

With my red vessel fully loaded with wooden gifts, I feel the wind picking up slightly and decide to head back home. I turn my kayak around very slowly, careful not to lose any of my haul and I am grateful the wind is at my back.

My paddling strokes are very short and choppy as the sticks strewn across my kayak hinder my ability to use a full stroke. It will take me longer to get back, but it is worth it. In the enjoyment of this morning's paddle, I rediscovered some long forgotten things about myself. The most important, I think, is to continually strive to use my creative talents. They are a vital component of who I am and bring me great joy. My shoreline sleuthing has been fun and full of interesting treasures. Nancy Drew would be proud!

Do you need to revisit a happy place back in your childhood?

Is there a memory of a time where you enjoyed something with so much passion that it makes you smile just thinking about it?

What clues can you discover about your life now?

Try to get out on the shoreline of your life today, recreate those moments for yourself and do a little sleuthing of your own!

Renewal

BIRTHDAY CELEBRATION

Renewal

*"Learn the pace of the universe
which is ever constant,
and seek not to race ahead or yet to drag behind.
A new day has been added to your experience."*
-Sam Campbell

BIRTHDAY CELEBRATION

I just love my birthday, don't you? I have dubbed June as birthday month" and each year I am excited to celebrate with family and friends.

I am a person of deep rituals and I have some special, annual "rites of birthday passage." First, I get up really early. My philosophy is that you can't ever have too many hours to relish on your birthday! This year I arise at 3:30 a.m. and put on a freshly brewed pot of my favorite Organic Wilderness Retreat coffee. I begin the day, as I do every day, with a spiritual reading, journaling and meditation. I am currently using a journal I received from my dear friend Jackie Messner for my birthday last year. The cover quote is by Henry David Thoreau, one of my personal favorites. It reads, "Our truest life is when we are in our dreams awake." I just love that.

I then go for my sunrise birthday run." It is invigorating to watch the sun peeking over the horizon to brighten "my" day. I return to enjoy a cup of coffee outside and open the cards and packages I have already received. I am deeply touched by the heart-warming and whimsical sentiments of family and friends and thank God for how blessed I am in my life. I even got a card in the mail from my dog, Bayfield! I wonder how that happened. I receive an early call from my loving mom, who always likes to be the first one to call on my birthday. My friend Mary Lavine calls singing the Polish birthday song, "Sto Lot," which is a wish to live 100 years. She practices the words by listening to some Polish choir and I must say, her rendition gets better each year.

As I leave for work, I notice a brightly colored "Happy Birthday" balloon on my porch and I know that my special friend Mary Kiser has been by. My business partner Jason Dobrzynski takes our work team out for a delicious lunch to one of my favorite haunts, Labriola's Café. My web designer Art Durham surprises me with a test run of my website, www.redkayak.net. My dear friend Mary Kay Walsh arranges a birthday get together of friends later in the week. A family gathering is planned for the upcoming weekend. Later in the day, my mom and my sister, Jan, leave a beautiful hanging basket of yellow and purple flowers on my front porch, and my friend Josette Songco gives me a handcrafted wicker basket filled with gifts for all my senses.

Given all these blessings, I ask myself, "How lucky can a person be?"

I pause in my celebratory day to think about how each birthday is a renewal. By staying open to the gifts of the day, my experiences are revitalizing. They offer a deeper meaning of time. Another calendar year passes, but my true rejuvenation is eternal. What can I gain from my new perspective of another year on the planet? How have I been renewed on this day? What truer essence is born today that enhances my purpose? These are deep questions that only require one thing - time on the water to ponder.

This is where my life-long friend and paddling buddy Janie Ford comes in. She agreed to go kayaking with me and late afternoon we met at Blackwell Forest Preserve to dip our paddles in the waters of 62-acre Silver Lake. It's an old quarry and is not a big body of water, but it gives us our kayaking "fix" and is a fabulous way to close out my birthday.

As always, Janie is prepared with all the special treats for our jaunt onto the water – first and foremost, homemade brownies (my favorite), Peanut Butter filled pretzels (whole grain, of course), Reese's Peanut Butter Cups®, Chocolate Brownie Clif® Bars (are you getting the chocolate/peanut butter connection?). And lots of bottles of water. You'd think we'd be paddling for days, but we believe you can never have too much food! She has the kayaks ready to launch by the time I arrive so we don't waste any time getting on the water. She takes care of everything!

It is a hot and humid 95° and thankfully there is a slight breeze as we start out. We slowly paddle some of the shoreline and enjoy seeing the Mallard ducks, Canadian geese, and red-winged blackbirds. Watching these different birds close out the day by ambling along the shore and resting on tree branches reminds me of the importance of taking time to peacefully end each day. I dont need to be racing 90 miles an hour from morning to night. There is a calmness of spirit that comes from taking our cues from the natural world.

There is a small island in the middle of this little treasure of a lake, which Janie has dubbed "Goose Island" for the goose eggs she has found there in late spring and early summer. We paddle over and spot white ones hidden up on a little ridge. The birth of a young gosling from an egg is truly one of nature's miracles and I feel a sense of serendipity seeing these eggs on my birthday. I reflect on the word "birth" and remind myself that not only on our birthdays, but every day we are being reborn. Each day we change ever so slightly, the cells in our bodies regenerate themselves and we are not the same person we were the day before.

Along with the subtle changes, there are often significant moments and events in our lives that transform us and challenge us to begin again. Our lives are in a constant state of regeneration and renewal. Life is a series of new beginnings and my birthday is a perfect reminder. We are born over and over again by life's experiences.

From the Great Blue Heron flying overhead to the little green frog on the bank and the purple coneflowers in bloom, our time on the water brings me back to that feeling of being centered with the universe and connected to the eternal continuum of time. What a gift! Closing out the day on the water is fabulous and I am grateful to Janie for making it happen.

Throughout this day I am reminded of the blessing of so many tremendously caring and giving people in my life who celebrate with me, not only on my birthday, but every day. As we "paddle on" through life together, I know that my journey would be empty without them. These extra-ordinary people, their constant caring, and their unconditional love – these are the greatest gifts of all for which I am deeply grateful.

Each day is a "birth" day of sorts. What special gifts of renewal have you received today?

What people make your life's journey special? Have you told them lately how grateful you are that they are sharing your life?

What "new beginning" is facing you and how will this change impact your days and months ahead?

Restoration

HUMANS AND NATURE

Restoration

"The call of the wild urges freedom over fear,
and after any time away in natural surroundings,
we go from being careful and appropriate
to daring and abandoned."
-Joan Anderson

HUMANS AND NATURE

It feels refreshing this July day to be back in Wisconsin. Since my yellow lab, Bayfield, had ACL surgery in May, we have been confined to spending her recovery time at home. Recently, her vet cleared her for more activity, so we venture north. I will reconnect with nature, and Bayfield will enjoy swimming and short hikes in the woods.

I am embroiled in the initial stages of a year-long work project and have been working seemingly non-stop since it began. I am amazed that in one month, this project has pulled me so far out of the essence of who I am. Without going into great detail, it is a mountain of paperwork that rubs against the grain of my ever-evolving ecological soul. I am cranky, frustrated and sense negativity creeping in, so it is time to go back to nature, to realign myself with my truth and bring some healing to my soul.

For me, time in nature is restorative, like a warm healing blanket that wraps itself around me and renders me whole. It is essential contemplative convalescence in nature's abbey.

After I arrive and rest a while, I begin to feel that "call" to the water. Sitting on the porch is no longer on my agenda – putting my paddle in the water is. The weather is warm, 83°, under a sunny, blue cloudless sky. The wind is calm and the UV Index is very high. Time to slather on some SPF 40 and go.

I exhale deeply as I push off from shore, as though I am trying to release all my recent stress in one long breath. Instantly, I begin to feel the rejuvenating power of the water. This is why I have come, to restore and renew and there is no better place for me than in my kayak.

I choose a route towards the railroad trestle that crosses the water at the shortest distance across the lake into a small quiet inlet. This waterway is very peaceful and calm, except when a train goes by! Near the trestle is a row of power lines, and I look up atthe Osprey nest perched on one of the towers. Then I see a Shell gas station sign on a pole on a little island, leaning precariously towards the water. Both have been there for many years.

While paddling, I think about the connection between humans and nature. The relationship is interesting – nature creates an island, humans erect power lines, and Ospreys build a nest on top. Nature creates an island, humans erect a gas station sign and grass and trees grow around it. The give and take between nature and humans is an ongoing encounter.

Paddling further into the inlet, I notice the very low water levels. When the water levels get really high, as they have been lately with heavy rainfall, the humans let water out of the lake through the dam and send it down river. The water stage is at least a foot below normal, and as I paddle into the little bay, I see the lily pads standing high like sentinels on guard, instead of gently resting on the water. They are still vibrantly blooming even though we have altered their normal supply of water. Nature provides us with ample rainfall, humans direct the course of the water and lily pads bloom.

Whenever I first arrive here and walk Bayfield, I pick wildflowers for the plastic water bottle I use as a "vase" for my table. I love to bring the seasonal bloom back home with me.

This ritual always reminds me of the John Denver song, Wildflowers in a Mason Jar. Its the story of him and his Grandpa riding on a bus through Georgia. His Grandpa recollects time on his Kentucky farm, the smell of rain and the feel of warm earth in his hands, relishing the memory of connecting to nature.

Paddling out of the inlet, I notice pretty purple Swamp Milkweeds to gather for my vase. When I get close to this beautiful, natural bouquet of flowers, I realize it is a haven for butterflies. Sitting quietly I watch the butterflies happily flitting around these flowers. I decide not to pick the flowers and take a few photos instead. A yellow and black Giant Swallowtail butterfly has been accompanying me in the inlet, fluttering about the shore. The instant I begin to photograph the flowers, she flew in behind me and landed on a purple flower right at the perfect snap of my shutter. She wanted in on the picture!

The Giant Swallowtail is one of NorthAmericas largest butterflies with an average wingspan of four to six inches. One of its distinctive characteristics is a yellow "eye"in each wing tail. Swamp Milkweeds are one of their favorite flowers.

I watch her dance around the flowers and it suddenly occurs to me that today is the anniversary of the passing of "Ma Oliver" – the dear, sweet Mother of my very special friends, Bev and Betsy Oliver. She was Mom to us all and loved butterflies. I believe the people we love who are no longer physically here offer us signs of their presence. I smile at the thought of "Ma Oliver" paddling with me, pluck a few reeds for my vase and continue on.

Paddling across the lake again, I notice the man-made concrete pylons holding the railroad trestle and again my thoughts turn to the relationship between humans and nature. I observe a little tree growing out of the concrete and shake my head in wonder. Humans put a concrete block in the water and trees grow inside.

In 2005, Richard Louv wrote a book titled *Last Child in the Woods* and introduced the term 'nature-deficit disorder' as a way to describe the growing gap between children and nature. His newest book, *The Nature Principle*, addresses this issue for adults. His quote so accurately reflects my current feelings of disconnect, "Electronic immersion without a force to balance it creates a hole in the boat, draining our ability to pay attention, think clearly, be productive and creative." Precisely why I am here.

My trip today is restorative. I feel some equilibrium returning to replenish me. I willingly accept nature's abundance to refresh and renew. Just being with her rescues my sagging spirit and repairs my tattered soul.

Paddling home I think about picking wildflowers and putting them in a plastic bottle – a real dichotomy of sorts, don't you think? Flowers and plastic, nature and humans. Although I recycle the plastic, perhaps I should get myself a mason jar.

It seems to me from my observations today, that regardless of the continual tug-of-war between humans and nature, nature always wins. In some fashion, she adapts to our endless assault and conforms to our often reckless abuse of the planet in the name of progress and development. I believe she will always stay one step ahead of us and will always be there for us to come back to – to reconnect and restore ourselves again.

Are you feeling out of balance in your everyday world?

Can you find some time away in the natural world to rejuvenate and restore?

What element of nature helps you to return to your equilibrium?

How can you find time today to restore yourself, and what can you give back to nature?

Truth
PLIGHT OF THE DAMSELFLY

Truth

*"A man is humble when he stands in the truth
with a knowledge and appreciation
for himself as he really is."*
~The Cloud of Unknowing

PLIGHT OF THE DAMSELFLY

Last night, Bayfield and I slept outside on the screen porch. The clear night sky was glorious and a gentle breeze blew in off the lake. I woke up to the early calls of the birds and the brightening sky of this July morning, feeling connected to the universe. The temperature was 63° and the wind was calm, a perfect morning for an early paddle.

I kayaked across the lake to the inlet my friends and I affectionately call 'the sanctuary." I have a feeling of reverence as enter this peaceful haven of wildlife. I was greeted by the loud trumpeting calls of the sand hill cranes and the twanging of a bull frog. A Great Blue Heron stood along the reeds welcoming me, while a Bald Eagle flew overhead. What a wonderful start to the day!

The lily pads were a thick green blanket on the water, like giant saucers covering a table. Paddling through these pads was a lot of work as my kayak moved sluggishly along. With each stroke I searched for a small open patch of water to dip my paddle. Once I got through the thickest area and reached a clearing in the water,

I sat back and was refreshed by the thought that this is the essence of who I am. I felt better reconnecting with nature.

As I rounded a turn in the inlet, there was an area of beautiful lilies in bloom standing in the water. I paddled over to take a few pictures and a baby damselfly landed on my arm. I smiled and said, "Good morning, little guy." He stayed a while and then started to crawl up my arm under my sleeve, and I gently brushed him to fly away. Well, my "gently" apparently was too much for him and instead of flying away, he landed in the water. I was horrified! Damselflies are not good swimmers, so I quickly scooped him up with the blade of my paddle and softly set him on my kayak. He appeared shaken and water logged, fluttering his wings to shake off the water. One of his wings was slightly bent at the end, perhaps from landing on the water.

I have come to have a real reverence for life, for all living creatures no matter how small. I believe that when a butterfly flaps its wings in the north, it alters the wind on some other side of this planet. The smallest, slightest change in nature has a large impact, whether we recognize it or can see it. To have disrupted the flight of this little damselfly this morning was incredibly painful to me.

I paddled over to a tree trunk in the water and gently set him down. I thought he could rest and regroup there and even have a bug or two to eat if he needed some extra energy, as aquatic insects are his primary diet. He was crawling around fairly well, but still not flying away. I could have cried. Freedom is very important to me and to think I may have unknowingly ended this little damselfly's ability to fly was crushing. I stayed with him for a long while and kept hoping he would fly away. As I watched him on the tree trunk, I fully realized how dainty and fragile his wings were. Delicate, intricate webbings of tiny threads. I felt just as fragile and horrible that in an instant, I had unintentionally ruined his morning... and mine, too.

So what really is this message? I think it is facing our own truth. Life is fragile like the damselflies' wings. We all unknowingly do things that have unintended consequences. We are human and we are not perfect. The connection of humans and nature is a continual give and take. Today I felt as though I took something from nature that was not mine. I also felt distraught writing about it. Who was I to disrupt this little damselfly's life? He was so innocent and seemed so happy and in an instant I ruined it.

I reluctantly left him there on the tree trunk, hoping that in time his wings would dry and he could fly away. All of a sudden, the "flow" of my morning was gone and I felt out of sync with everything. I began to cry. I cried again writing about it. That little damselfly touched me so deeply. How often do our good intentions go awry?

Recognizing our own truths is not always easy. Revealing and accepting both our good traits and our faults Is both painful and liberating. Acknowledging our failures is a personal challenge in honesty. Owning them helps us to swallow the ego of who we think we are, to become truthful about what is. This is the recognition that frees us. The morning's damselfly experience reminded me that I am not always as gentle and reverent of things as I strive to be. Hard to accept, but it is the truth.

As I paddled back across the lake, another little damselfly took rest on the front hull of my kayak and accompanied me home. As I approached the shore, an adult dragonfly, the damselfly's cousin, flew right next to me, about a foot away from the left side of my head. I am especially fond of dragonflies because they represent transformation. She hovered for a few fluttering moments and then was off, staying long enough to meet my gaze with her big, bulging eyes. She reminded me of the elusive Golden Snitch, that golden ball with silver wings in the fictional Wizarding sport Quidditch played in the Harry Potter movies. As I pulled up on shore, the little damselfly alighted, off to explore some new territory.

I dont know what those two were trying to tell me. Maybe they were saying, "you stupid careless human disrupting nature" or maybe they were letting me know the little guy would be fine. I am not going to try to interpret their message. All I know is there is a part of me that wants to paddle back to that tree trunk to see if he is gone, if he could muster the ability to fly. And there is a part of me that doesn't; because he may be struggling or even dead on that tree trunk, and I didn't want to see it. I felt bad enough.

Why has this touched me so deeply? Because I was reminded that paddling is neutral; it's the experiences on the water, both good and bad, that bring home the lessons of life. I had to receive the unpleasant message from this damselfly, accept the consequences, and stand in my own truth. I felt I had been part of the disruption of nature that I abhor.

At first, I felt this episode only added to the disconnectedness I have been feeling over this last month. But as I reflected on this experience further, I realized that perhaps I hurt so badly because of my connectedness to nature. If I were truly disconnected, I would not feel such deep loss and grief. I think my damselfly teacher resurrected unprocessed grief from other losses in my life and touched a chord of truth I had not previously faced.

I truly hope he will be all right and I must trust that this happened for a reason. I have learned a great lesson in truthfulness today from that tiny damselfly. Sometimes the biggest, and the toughest lessons, come from unexpected little places.

Have you done something lately you are not especially proud of?

Has something occurred that you would rather not talk about and rather not accept?

What one thing do you need to do, right now, to stand in your own truth?

Are there any uncomfortable, hidden truths lurking within that need to surface?

If so, grab a really good friend or your favorite journal and get it out there. It won't change what happened, but it will teach you a lesson and help you to do better next time.

Stewardship
JUNK BARGE

Photo by Ann Moss

Stewardship

"Man did not weave the web of life.
He is merely a strand in it.
Whatever he does to the web,
he does to himself."

- Chief Seattle

JUNK BARGE

On this calm, overcast August morning, I am heading out with my friends Janie Ford, Ann Moss and Josette Songco to paddle for a few hours at Blackwell Forest Preserve on 62-acre Silver Lake. Our purpose for paddling is to get Ann on her maiden kayaking voyage and Josette out for the first time this year. We are preparing for our paddling excursion in Sedona, Arizona, in September and the four of us have planned to connect on the water in anticipation of our trip.

Our pre-launch begins with a check of our food supply. It doesn't seem to matter if we are going out for a day or a few hours, food inventory is always a high priority. As always, we are well stocked for our time on the water.

We begin our paddle out to the left shoreline where the tall, green reeds greet us and the Mallard ducks amble around on the sand. We are out only 45 minutes when we take our first food break. We are pathetic, but the homemade brownies are just too much to resist. After our quick snack, we all head off in slightly different directions with the battle cry, "until we eat again...."

Under a slight drizzle, we discover how nice it is sometimes to be out on the water in the rain. The light rainfall seems to soften everything. As I paddle along, I scan the shoreline for refuse. My friends and I, among many things, share a commitment to stewardship when we are on the water. I begin to pick up miscellaneous debris – plastic cups, water bottles, cans and a collection of bobbers of various shapes and colors.

Time to eat again and we stop at a shoreline spot with easy access to a picnic table. Within an instant the table is covered with goodies ranging from brownies, chips, Chex Mix™, crackers and peanut butter to various types of fruit.

After our break, we paddle toward the right side of the lake. I find more debris on the shoreline and everyone began to call my kayak the "junk barge." The old gym shoe and moldy green tennis ball on the pile made everyone laugh. It prompted me to do a little research on stewardship when I got home.

According to Wikipedia, in its purest sense, stewardship is an ethic that embodies responsible planning and management of resources and is linked to the concept of sustainability. Historically, stewardship was the responsibility given to household help to bring food and drinks to a castle dining hall. It later expanded to all household and domestic affairs and then became the responsibility of taking care of passengers on ships, trains, planes and in restaurants. What struck me is that in any context, stewardship revolved around taking care of something or somebody.

Environmental stewardship is an important part of time in my kayak. It's about taking care of my surroundings, taking care of the space I inhabit – "leave no trace" as we say in nature. Leave it all as you found it. And if we can leave it better than we found it, then that has even more value.

After all, we are responsible for our own personal stewardship and the impact of our physical presence on the environment. Do we really need one more _____? You fill in the blank. Our closets are bursting with unworn clothes. Workplaces are overflowing with cabinets of files and paper. (When was it that we went "paperless?") People's living spaces are being overrun with clutter. As a result, businesses are springing up everywhere to help people manage the pile of stuff they accumulate.

I recently did an exercise in ridding myself of physical possessions by pretending I was moving. I asked myself this question, "If I were moving, would I take this item with me?" If the answer was no, I recycled or donated it. I was even brave enough to throw out four boxes that were in my attic for 18 years without opening them. Once I was finished I felt lighter. But then I looked around and realized I could do it all over again. Amazing. My "junk barge" reminded me I better go through the process again.

We didn't stop to eat anymore. Thank goodness since we were only out on the water for three hours!

We enjoyed a nice, quiet morning paddle, the soft sunlight streaming to the clear bottom of the lake. Four friends sharing a sacred space of time on the water. A perfect way to start the day along with the reward of a cleaner shoreline. So, "until we eat again," I ask you:

Are there possessions in your life that you need to get rid of?

What things, people, circumstances or emotions would you pick up and put on your own "junk barge"?

If you could take one action of personal stewardship today, what would that be? Do it!

Sustenance

SILENCE AND WILD RICE

Sustenance

"Human beings are of such natures
that they should have not only material facilities
but spiritual sustenance as well.
Without spiritual sustenance, it is difficult
to get and maintain peace of mind."
~ Dalai Lama

SILENCE AND WILD RICE

It's August and I am happy to write that I am in my beloved northwoods of Wisconsin. The feeling of coming 'home again' stirs in my soul and I treasure each and every moment I spend here. I become refreshingly alive and fully engaged in the woods and the water surrounding me.

This morning is my first paddle on Wild Rice Lake, a 375-acre lake that is part of the ten-lake Manitowish Chain. My family has been coming to Copps' Cabins, a resort on this lake, since I was ten years old and every year this northern trek provides much needed renewal for me.

On this crisp morning, I walk down to the sandy shoreline with a spring in my step and say out loud to no one in particular, "Oh, yeah!" The perfectly calm lake is waiting to embrace me, like the warm hug of an old friend I haven't seen in a while.

My tradition for this first paddle is kayaking my favorite section of the Trout River. I visit this river every year through many different conditions, and always look forward to the lessons it teaches me each time I return. This undeveloped stretch of river cuts through tall reeds and is graced on each side by wooded land. Until I reach the cranberry bogs of the Trout River Cranberry Company, no sounds of human activity interrupt the quiet.

The water levels on the lake are exceptionally high, and I anticipate an easy paddle. As I enter the river from the lake, I quickly notice how wide the water has cut through the reeds. Normally, the river width is about six feet, but today the river is twice as wide. This expanded stretch of water creates new pathways around interesting clumps of reeds, which I dub "reed islands" and I venture in and around them like I am on some expedition. How fun!

Suddenly, I notice the absolute quiet. This area of the river is normally peaceful, but this morning it seems exceptionally silent. Maybe it is or maybe it only seems that way because I am so in need of silence. Whatever the reason, I relish it, sit back, gently paddle and let it seep into my soul. The warmth of the morning sun only enhances my tranquility and I close my eyes to just "be" in this monastery of stillness.

I experience the comforting blanket of the great silence that Sigurd F. Olson writes about in *Reflections from the North Country*. He writes, "The great silences mean more than stillness. They are the ancient overpowering silences this planet knew before the advent of modern man."

This "great silence" accompanies me as I paddle further, becoming acutely aware of my senses and my vivid perception of the wildness around me. The clarity of the flora and fauna along the riverbank emerges, like putting a camera lens into sharp focus. Just as the wider waterway expands my ability to kayak into new areas, I, too, was opening to the blessings of this morning's paddle, going deeper into my own soul, into my inner core. The utter quiet allows a sense of repair to return to my spirit and presents the gift of inward healing that comes from spending time in nature's rhythm.

Meandering around these "reed islands" I become mesmerized by their intricate structure and shape with wild rice clutching them, like the last leaves of autumn clinging to the trees. Having spent many years paddling this river, I realize how little I know about the wild rice that grows here and gives the lake its name. It would be an interesting topic to write about back at the cabin. And then I say to myself, "Hello! Who really cares about wild rice and reeds?" I think they're pretty cool as I weave in and out of these clumps of aquatic grass, but who else would really care?

Paddling on, a notion occurs to me. What might the two profound observances of the morning – the silence and the reeds with wild rice – have in common? Is there a subtle thread between these two distinctly different elements of nature? After all, aren't all things in the natural world somehow connected?

And then it strikes me. Sustenance is what they have in common. Sustenance for both the soul and the body.

Silence is the spiritual sustenance. To quote Olsons book further, he writes, "When man feels tension as though he were being pulled out of his ancient mold, it is his divorcement from silence that is often responsible, silence built into the fabric of his mind. He may not know what is wrong, but he only has to find it again to restore his equilibrium."Silence. The Voice of the Wilderness. Sustenance for the soul.

The wild rice and reeds have their own story. Years ago, and still today, many Native Americans and others harvest the wild rice by canoeing into a stand of reeds. One person "knocks" the rice grain heads into the canoe with poles called 'knockers" while the other person slowly paddles. A sacred ritual in tune with the seasons of nature.

Wild rice is a popular staple because of its superior nutritional value and taste. High in protein, fiber and many minerals, it provides necessary nourishment. Sustenance for the body. A staple in ancient and modern cultures.

This interesting connection from my time on the river this morning reminds me that I need the balance of sustaining both my body and soul. I need to be continually conscious of the importance of maintaining that healthy equilibrium. There is a deep connection between both physical and spiritual well being. I need to create the space for sustenance in my life to allow transformation of my inner landscape.

My grandmother, Mary, who passed away at age 101, always used to say, "If you don't have your health, you don't have anything." She was a wise woman who understood the importance of sustenance.

The *American Heritage Dictionary* defines sustenance as the supporting of life or health, nourishment, food; a means of support. Today on the river, I have found sustenance.

What things, people or places in your life provide sustenance for your body and soul?

What elements of your life nourish you and how can you minimize or eliminate those that deplete you? Who supports you?

Where do you go to find your silence, your sustenance for your soul? And how do you choose to nourish your body?

Can you carve out some time today for your own personal sustenance?

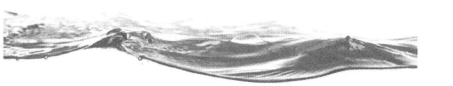

Being Present

EAGLE'S FEATHER

Being Present

"You must live in the present, launch
yourself on every wave,
find your eternity in each moment."
- Henry David Thoreau

EAGLE'S FEATHER

On a beautiful August morning in the northwoods of Wisconsin I was blessed with a special gift of a trip to Dam Lake in St. Germain to kayak with my friend, Marianne Sullivan. A novice paddler, she was spending the week nearby with her family. She invited me to spend some time on the water, and although I am always grateful for the opportunity to paddle a new stretch of lake, I was more excited about kayaking with Marianne as we never paddled together before.

The temperature was 75° and the wind was fairly strong and we began to kayak with the tailwind and explore the shoreline. At first, our conversation was light, and we talked about things we have been doing since we both arrived in the northwoods and our plans for the remainder of the week. And then, as it always does after a short time on the water, our talk moved to a deeper level.

It never ceases to amaze me how quickly paddling and being on the water gets to the soul, allowing intimate thoughts and feelings to surface. For some reason, there is a sense on the water that you can talk about anything. Everything is fair game and nothing is judged or criticized. The liberating feeling of paddling in rhythm with another frees the heart from what has been locked inside. I have learned about the innermost ponderings of so many people just paddling side by side.

For me, it comes from the feeling of being present when I am on the water. Nothing else is as important as what is happening at that moment. I think that feeling of being in attendance with a fellow paddler lends itself to deeper conversation more quickly. When I am truly present and listening to someone, the connection is authentic and the conversation is genuine. Any counterfeit masks fall away.

As we turned around and paddled into the headwind, we talked about life and loss, and moving forward. We learned more about each other and our lives. I have found that once you paddle with someone, your relationship is forever deepened because of the intimacy of the conversation, the sharing of inner truths and the willingness to be open and render yourself vulnerable. It's all about being present to another.

We kayaked until we reached a slight turn in the shoreline and the headwind increased. After a few minutes of dipping our paddles in and out of the water and realizing we were going nowhere, we laughed and decided it was time to turn around and head back home.

As we approached the pier, we spotted a magnificent Bald Eagle in the tall evergreen tree at the shoreline. With the forceful wind at the top of this pine tree he swayed back and forth, hanging on for dear life.

The Bald Eagle, being the national symbol of freedom for the United States ofAmerica since 1782, is an amazing bird of prey. They are powerful fliers averaging 20-40 m.p.h. and can reach speeds of 100 m.p.h. during a dive. They can also swim which comes in handy as their diet is primarily fish. There are stories of Bald Eagles that grasp a heavy fish in their mouth and swim quite a distance to land to enjoy their catch on the shore. Eagles live 20-30 years in the wild, generally mate for life and return to the same nesting area every year. Surprisingly, they have about 7,000 feathers.

Bald Eagles are a common sight in the northwoods during the summer. I have often wondered why they are called "bald" since they are not, and I learned that the name "bald" is from an obsolete English word meaning white. Who knew?

Finding eagle feathers on the water and land here is not unusual. As Marianne, her family and I watched this eagle cling to the branch with all the might his knife-like talons could muster, what we witnessed next was truly uncommon.

We saw one of his 7,000 feathers leave his body and despite the gusty winds, float ever so gently down to the water, as if in slow motion. This feather's journey from limb to lake was suspended in time. We instinctively knew we were given a special gift and after the feather softly landed in the water, no one spoke. We sat in silence, relishing this blessing, this holy experience a moment longer. In the sacred stillness of this witness, we were fully present.

NativeAmerican interpretations of the meaning of finding an eagle's feather vary, but in most tribes, it is held in high regard, and only Chiefs are allowed to wear them. Some tribes think it is a good luck omen and others feel it is their personal totem.

For me on this day, it represented the good fortune of paddling with Marianne and sharing one of those rare gifts of nature that I often experience on the water.

I was also reminded that we don't always have to travel very far to find life's treasures. Today we paddled up and down the shoreline only to find nature's most memorable gift at the doorstep of their beach.

This experience made me think about how often I find myself searching for something more, where the grass is greener, or in the paddling sense, where the water is bluer and calmer. I often forget the "now" as I continually project myself into the future, anticipate the new and ponder my next steps. The blessing of the eagle's feather was a present, and it brought me to the present.

Often in moments when we are awestruck by the majesty of nature we return more fully to our true selves, our authentic nature. We recycle back to our very essence. It is the power of the "now" moment and all we really have. Very often, we don't have to travel or paddle too far to capture these moments and in some slight way, become inherently changed by the experience.

The eagle's feather taught me vital lessons to carry forward. 'Be in the moment. Be observant. Be fully present.'

What gifts are waiting for you today outside your door?

Can you take a moment, to stop and be fully present and let nature provide a whisper of your essence?

How can you, in your daily life, concentrate on fully participating in the moments? Today, don't miss them, just be with them.

Expansion
LOONY PADDLERS

Expansion

> "Ever since I was a child I have had this
> instinctive urge for expansion and growth.
> To me, the function and duty
> of a quality human being
> is the sincere and honest development
> of one's potential."
> ~Bruce Lee

LOONY PADDLERS

All summer long my mom has been reading the postings in a local newspaper, following the weekly outings of a group of women kayakers in northern Wisconsin called The Loony Paddlers. These excursions are organized by Kit Bogenschneider, who does it purely for the pleasure of getting women out on the water and forming new friendships of women who love to kayak.

The group is called The Loony Paddlers because of the Common Loon, which is so prevalent in the north in the summer. Loons have difficulty walking on land because their legs are set far back on their bodies and are more at home on the water. So it is a fitting name for this crew that takes to the water each week.

Before myAugust vacation to the northwoods, I contacted Kit to see if I might join them while I was there. She was more than happy to have me come along, and I was grateful for the chance to kayak with new people and explore a different stretch of water.

The itinerary for this trip was to put in at Island Lake on the Manitowish Chain of Lakes, paddle through Island, Spider and Stone Lakes and take out near the Rest Lake Dam. It was a beautiful morning with plentiful sunshine and fairly calm winds. I relish a new adventure and after meeting everyone before we launched, I knew this was going to be a great morning with kindred spirits on the waters in my beloved northwoods.

As we paddled along, I listened to the conversations of these women, and realized that most of them did not know each other before they began these weekly jaunts to the lakes and rivers of the north. Women who were strangers have now become friends. I tried to spend a little time with each person, to share a bit of our stories and our love of kayaking.

It was fitting that about mid-way through this four-hour trip, we came upon a pair of loons on Stone Lake. Loons are multi-talented birds. In addition to being able to fly up to 75 m.p.h., loons have the ability to dive more than 250 feet underwater and stay there for as long as five minutes. Their red eyes help them to see more clearly underneath the surface.

One of the most fascinating motions I have ever seen a loon perform is when it stretches its wings, lifts its bill and neck to the sky, and flaps vigorously for a few seconds while balancing on the water. It is as if it is trying to expand its whole being and open itself up to the world. As I watched one of these loons on Stone Lake perform this ritual, I looked around at my fellow paddlers and realized that in a sense, this is what they have done. Reached out and opened themselves to one another, not knowing what the result would be. Kit, by graciously extending her weekly invitation to all who wished to share time on the water, has provided the pathway, the waterway, for new friendships.

I think there is a great lesson in all of this. Like the loon extending its wings on the water, these women have done the same. And isn't that truly the way to add richness to our lives? To continue to expand and grow and be willing to encounter the new? To extend ourselves to others, even those we don't know? These women who were once strangers have now become friends. They broke through their cocoon of safety and security to venture into the unknown. Within the newness of their friendship, they also experience new waters. A double bonus of opportunity to seek and grow and share.

Continuing to expand and grow is an important piece of our own development as human beings. So many people just stop, thinking that they are either too old or too afraid to venture into the new. What a sad place to be. The universe waits patiently for us to make our way into the unknown. How exciting would it be if we look at our lives as a daily exercise in welcoming change from what has become stale and familiar? No matter how small or seemingly insignificant, every step we take towards the new and exciting leads to more of the same. Just as exercising our muscles on a regular basis makes them stronger, spreading our own wings like the loon a little each day could lead to exciting discoveries and bigger adventures.

I applaud The Loony Paddlers for the weekly expansion of their kayaking horizons and the nourishing of their budding friendships. I am grateful to have shared a day's journey.

What areas of your life need a little expansion?

Are there any stale circumstances that need to be freshened up with a new discovery?

Is there one thing you can do today, to expand yourself in an area that needs a little more attention?

Friendship
DUCKY KAYAKS

Photo by Chris Fuselier

Friendship

> "Friendship is the grace
> that warms and sweetens our lives:
> Nobody would choose to live without friends
> even if he had all other good things."
> ~Aristotle

DUCKY KAYAKS

I looked forward to this September trip to Sedona, Arizona, with mixed anticipation. I was excited to remember my friend Mary winning this trip at the spring luncheon in April, the book signing with Joan, and the incredible energy of that day. My feelings were mixed because this was the same time of year when I lost "Mary" Jan Malloy, my paddling partner, and the anniversary of her wake and funeral. In one sense, it was hard to imagine this trip during this time frame. In another, it was so fitting. Years ago, she bought me Joan's first book, *A Year by the Sea*, for my birthday. I remember her saying to me, "I think you will like this author. You like this stuff!" I took the book with me on a weekend to Wisconsin and could not put it down. Twelve years later, a new found friendship with Joan, the book signing and the trip to Sedona at this time, well, the serendipity of it all spoke for itself.

With high energy and anticipation, the Sedona Seven, as we dubbed ourselves, Angela Anello, Janie Ford,

Mary Lavine, Deb Maschmeier, Ann Moss, Josette Songco and I, formulated our trip plans. Energetic emails about flight arrangements, arrival times, and yes, the food were zooming across computer screens. I was determined to kayak and found just the perfect excursion through Sedona Adventure Tours. Most people don't go to Sedona to kayak, but we are different. We look for the adventure of things and this was certainly going to be a memorable one – paddling the Verde River in Ducky Kayaks. What?? Sounded like great fun to me!

The Verde River is nestled in the Camp Verde Valley, and the meeting place for this trip was about 40 miles southeast of Sedona at a place called Beasley Flats. What?? Beasley Flats! Sounds like some place out of an old Western movie. I can just hear the cowboys saying, "Hey, let's head over this pass to Beasley Flats and park our horses. Get some grub." Here's that food thing again! Well the itinerary said, "Included with your river adventure are snacks and bottled water." Right up our alley!

Anyway, the driving directions captured that same essence - "turn right at Salt Mine Road" and then "turn left at the end of the pavement." We really felt like we were in the middle of nowhere. We even stopped once to check to see if we were going the right way. What?? How could we know? Salt mines to the right and tumbleweeds and scraggly turf to the left. Paddle on, I guess!

I can appreciate these adventures most when sharing them with my friends. The seven of us on this trip are at various stages of friendship, some lifelong and some brand new. No matter. True friendship emerges instantly when you are with people you can be genuine with. No pretense, no masks. We just all truly care about each other as human beings with all our great traits and foolish faults. To be with my friends on this journey is the best part of the trip.

We arrived at a small parking lot, sparsely adorned with a bathroom building and a few trash cans, and we figured we were in the right place. This, apparently, was Beasley Flats. What?? No gettin' grub here. Just to make sure, I called Sedona Adventure Tours. "Oh yes," the woman said. "Your river guides are on their way." OK.

As if on cue, our guides, Chris and Greg, arrived with the shuttle vans to take us to the put in, the starting point for any excursion on a river. We were to receive our safety talk, get fitted with our Personal Flotation Devices and then launch.

These "Ducky Kayaks" were something I had never seen before. Large, inflatable vessels that looked more like giant footballs sliced in half. What??

The itinerary for the trip detailed many of the rapids and bends on the river. We ran Clear Creek Rapids, we glided down the "S" shaped Tunnel of Love, floated around Butterfly Bend, ran the Rocky Rapids and cruised beneath the Cliffs of Insanity. Cliffs of Insanity? What?? Where were we anyway?

Paddling a calm stretch, then some rapids, then a calm stretch again, then more rapids was the mantra and pulse of this river. It was exhilarating paddling this way, especially in these rubbery Ducky Kayaks. As we cruised through the rapids, we bounced off the rocks, spun around, and sometimes came through the rapids backwards, laughing the entire way. "Interspersed with exhilarating chutes and calm floating pools, the Verde is the perfect river experience for folks of all ages," read the itinerary. Indeed it was.

I must digress here a moment and go back to the food. On the Southwest Airlines flight to Phoenix, our infectious enthusiasm for this trip caught on with the flight attendants. We told them we were going kayaking and needed snacks for the trip. In addition to the traditional bag of peanuts, they showered us with cute little packages of Cheese Nips® and Oreo® cookies. So periodically on our journey down the Verde, someone would yell, "Cheese Nips®!" and these little yellow packages would emerge from Janie's dry bag. The guides thought we were crazy! What??

The collective sharing of these fun-filled moments provides the continual building blocks of honest friendship – creating memories from silly things, laughing and sharing with each other. We all need these friends in our lives. It is a lonely journey without them.

Finally, no trip on the river is ever complete without someone going in. Deb, an experienced kayaker, had the honors of baptism in the Verde. Our tour guides had given each of us a bilge pump turned into a squirt gun for some fun on the river. Deb's inner child was shouting, "Hooray! Squirt gun fight!" and during the course of our time on the river had managed to douse everyone, except Josette.

In her own words, Deb writes, "I knew Josette had an expensive 35mm camera and I was fearful of soaking that camera in my quest to drench her. I advised her to tuck her camera away so it would not get wet in the upcoming rapids. As she pulled away, I drew river water into my "gun," aimed and fired. A direct bull's-eye! As she paddled downstream, she mumbled something about being ambushed, but my inner child felt triumphant."

Moments later, as Deb approached a huge rock in the rapids, she found herself suddenly submerged under water. As she struggled to gain her footing and retrieve her kayak and paddle, it was Josette who paddled back to help her. Poetic justice or the strengthening bonds of friendship on the water? I'll let you decide.

In his beautifully written book, *Anam Cara*, John ODonohue explores the Celtic understanding of love and friendship. He writes, "… your friendship cuts across all convention, morality, and category. You are joined in an ancient and eternal way with the 'friends of your soul."

The essence of this trip and kayaking adventure is all about that level of authentic friendship. I have the greatest amigos in the world. These are people who I am myself with, who understand me and I them. We have paddled through many highs and lows together in our lives. In everything, we share our deepest feelings and our highest aspirations. We help each other to live better lives. And we love each other through it all. For them, for this trip, for this time together, I am truly grateful.

Who are your friends? Who are the people you turn to in times of celebration and sorrow?

Who are the people that sustain you, nourish your growth and encourage you on your journey?

Today, pick up the phone and call one of them and tell them how grateful you are that they are in your life.

Cleansing
ROCK RIVER SWEEP

Cleansing

"If everyone sweeps their own doorstep,
the whole world would be clean."

-Anonymous

ROCK RIVER SWEEP

I have always wanted to do an "official" river sweep. Even though I do my stewardship on the water when I paddle, I had hoped to join a group whose sole purpose for the day was to clean up a stretch of riverbank.

This September day, I found myself participating in the 2nd Annual Rock River Sweep in Rockford, Illinois, and the clean-up of a section of this 276 mile river. I hoisted my red kayak on the car and packed my dry bag with food and a few bottles of water for the day. I smiled as I tossed in a few extra packages of Cheese Nips® and Oreos® left over from our excursion on the Verde River in Sedona 10 days ago.

The Rock River is one of the main tributaries to the Mississippi, and starts in the Theresa Marsh near Theresa, Wisconsin, in the southeast part of the state, about 17 miles south of Fond du Lac. It flows southwest through Wisconsin and then into the northwest corner of Illinois where it picks up the Kishwaukee River and then joins the Mississippi at Rock Island. I enjoy learning a little about the river I am paddling.

I arrived promptly at the meeting area in Blackhawk Park, named for the Sauk nation and their famous warrior leader, Chief Blackhawk. In the 1800s, the Blackhawk War took place on this river and raged over many counties in Illinois and Wisconsin. My assignment was to clean a stretch of the South Rockford Reach beginning near the Fordham Dam with my new paddling buddies, Stewart and John. We left our kayaks at the put in where we would start our paddle and then drove in procession to leave our cars at the take out. I smiled at the sight of our vehicles with empty roof racks of various sizes and shapes and colors. We looked like a human herd of deer heading down the road. We humans are always trying to emulate nature!

We left our cars parked at the Hinchcliff Forest Preserve and ambled into the shuttle that will take us back to our various starting points. I relaxed back in my seat, closed my eyes, listened to the lively chatter among the paddlers and thought to myself, "These are my people." My people! I didn't even know anyone. Yet we are fellow paddlers who not only share a love of kayaking, but also care of the environment, giving back and doing our part to keep our waterways clean.

As I listened to the spirited conversations, I noticed that everyone talked about different aspects of kayaking. They were not talking about what they do, where they work, or their families. They were all sharing stories about kayaking trips and time spent on the water. I smiled to myself. Paddling is the great equalizer, I decided. I might be with the head of an international company, people who are retired or college students. No matter. It's all about sharing our love of being on the water.

This is how life should be, I thought. We are all human, all trying our best to make our way during our time on this planet. Our judgments and evaluations of others really have no place if we are to truly live a peaceful life. The tranquility of this notion filled my heart as we jolted around in the shuttle bus and arrived at our starting point.

As we prepared our launch onto the swirling waters of the Rock River, Stewart shared some fun gifts with me. He gave me the coolest white rubbery boots to slosh around on the murky banks. He also loaned me a tool called a Telescopick to easily snatch smaller pieces of debris from the shoreline without leaving my kayak. It reminded me of the occupational therapy tool nurses give to patients to help them grab out of reach items.

I was amazed at how much garbage was on the shoreline as we began our clean-up operation. Glass and plastic bottles, candy wrappers, broken glass, plastic bags, articles of clothing. What a mess! I have a great time plucking debris off the shoreline with my Telescopick. Like dumpster diving without having to go in the dumpster. Was I crazy to be enjoying cleaning up other people's garbage?

I was surprised at how quickly we filled bag after bag with the shoreline refuse. John found an empty bucket and filled that with trash as well. It was difficult to paddle loaded down with bags of rubbish and challenging to navigate the swift moving current. I thought about how often in life we get bogged down with emotional garbage, both our own and other peoples. How many times in our lives should we be moving along with the current and going with the flow of things, and yet we allow ourselves to be slowed down or stopped by all the emotional debris we carry. Just like the river bank, we need cleansing, too.

Some of the more interesting shoreline finds were a horseshoe, cell phone and white plastic chair that Stewart found and affixed to the front his kayak like a throne! I told him he was really doing his "Stewart"ship with that chair and John thought it was good luck that I found a horseshoe. But I was thinking, "Where does all this stuff come from?"

We made a few stops to drop our garbage bags in the dumpsters at sites along the river. I felt good about my stewardship knowing I had given something back to the rivers that offer us so much.

Paddling back to the take out, Stewart and John were engaged in conversation, and I was engaged in deep thought. I was thinking about garbage. Mine and other peoples.

I just spent the last few hours of my life cleaning up other people's garbage, and I thought how often in our day to day lives do we do that. How frequently do we ask other people to do that for us, willingly or not? I'm not talking about physical stuff; Im talking about the emotional baggage we all carry around with us from past experiences, hurts and regrets. Garbage that we drag around with us as if it will serve some useful purpose in the future. Things like unresolved anger, judgment, bitterness, unforgiveness and resentment. How much does this debris weigh us down and how much does it impair our relationships? If we filled trash bags with that stuff how many would we have? Wouldnt we rather clean it all up and have a pristine shoreline of our own?

I remembered reading a great book by Richard J. Leider and David A. Shapiro titled *Repacking Your Bags: Lighten Your Load for the Rest of Your Life*. One question they raised about both physical and emotional baggage was; "Does all this make you happy?" What a great question to ask about all the garbage in our lives.

This really brought some good insight to me. To periodically take inventory of our emotional debris and give it a good cleansing is one of the healthiest things we can do.

Participating in the Rock River Sweep reminded me of my responsibility to take care of my own garbage, to clear out the emotional debris from my life, and to recycle myself again and again. To create something new out of the old that will allow me to move forward and participate more fully in my life.

What is the garbage in your life? Is it yours or someone else's? Or both?

Have you knowingly given your baggage to someone else to carry and have you willingly taken someone else's?

Does all your extra stuff, both physical and emotional, really make you happy?

What cleansing steps do you need to take in your life to sweep your own riverbank? What one thing can you do today?

Closure
LAST PADDLE

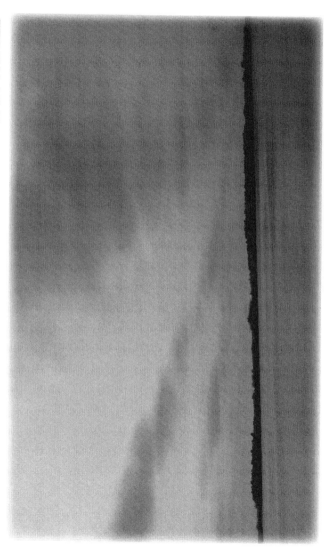

Closure

"As we pay attention
to the wisdom we carry within us –
the wisdom of heart, mind, and body;
the wisdom of our dreams and our passions –
we will discern the unique way of living
that is ours for this season of our lives."

-Nancy L. Bieber

LAST PADDLE

One of my many paddling rituals is to begin and end the paddling season with a solo paddle in my trusty little red Aqueterra kayak. The kayak that has been with me through all of my paddling seasons.

In October in Wisconsin, the weather is uncertain. With the temperature hovering around 50° and a pretty strong ENE wind gusting to 20 miles per hour, I wasn't sure if I'd get a chance to go out and paddle again if I didn't go now.

The water is calm on my side of the lake, so I pull out my red kayak and say, "C'mon little vessel, time for us to hit the water one more time."

The sights are spectacular. The final faint hint of the fall colors adorns the shoreline. The river birch trees hold on to the last of their yellow leaves. The evergreens stand firm, ready for winter's embrace. There is a hazy sun breaking through the clouds, providing just enough sunlight to warm the day. It is on days like these I feel like I could paddle forever and let my thoughts flow free.

When Bayfield, my yellow lab, had her surgery in the spring, I wasnt sure how my paddling season would unfold, if at all. I approached this year without high expectations, and it has turned out to be a really amazing and fun season on the water.

Along with some great solo paddles in familiar places, I kayaked with different people on new bodies of water. Reflecting back on this season, I realize that many things have come full circle.

The quote at the beginning of this book is the ending quote of my first book. This year I stepped into many diverse waters and I am not the same person that I was at the beginning of this season.

I recognize how fitting it was to finish my last major paddle of the season in Rockford, where this "season on the water" began in April with the book signing at the luncheon with Joan. It will finish with parting thoughts in December as I travel to visit her on Cape Cod. I could not script this season with a more serendipitous ending.

I read an excerpt titled "Close to Home" in an issue of *Canoe and Kayak* magazine. Author Jeff Moag writes about paddling in many places, but his "flat-out best paddling" days were spent on The Potomac. His home river. "The Potomac River taught me how to paddle," he concludes.

For me, Castle Rock Lake is my home water. The place where I begin and end every season and have so many insightful paddling trips in between. It's the water that buoys me as I learn many of my deepest life lessons.

What is the importance of this paddle today? It brings closure to the season. It is my own ritual of looking back, reflecting on my many kayaking excursions and closing this paddling chapter. This paddle connects all the adventures of this season for me, like smaller rivers converging into a larger one. Even the distinctive cloud patterns today appear as billowy pathways radiating to one place in the flattened sky.

I think we do not do this as often as we should in our lives. How often do we, after seemingly insignificant occurrences or major life events, sit back and ponder and bring closure? It is an important part in our growth process that is so often overlooked. We rush headlong from one thing to the next and miss this critical step in between. This process of honoring the conclusion of one phase of our lives and transitioning to the beginning of the next is necessary if we are to fully open ourselves to the new. It is an invaluable, essential pause and without it, everything just runs together in one endless stream of busyness. We must remember that the blessings that await us are not dependent on our pace.

Envision crossing a bridge over a swift flowing river. More than likely, we stop on the bridge to look at the water below. We look back at where we have just come from and then view the new scenery on the other side. This is the pause, the suspension on the bridge, the intermission if you will, between the old and the new.

That's what this last paddle is for me. Reflecting back over the season, spending this quiet contemplative time on the water and then heading back to shore, putting closure to this kayaking season. It's about coming full circle on my home water.

What parts of your life need closure?

Are there circumstances or events in your life that you need to review and then let go?

How can you carve out time today to pause, look back and then let go of one thing that no longer serves you?

What is holding you back from closure of the old to the unfolding of the new?

Parting Thoughts
TIDES AND SEASONS

Parting Thoughts

"The ocean is one of the delights
for the human eye.
The seashore is a theater of fluency.
When the mind is entangled,
it is soothing to walk by the seashore,
to let the rhythm of the ocean inside you."
- John O'Donohue

TIDES AND SEASONS

Each day I am on Cape Cod I walk the beach at low tide when the seas buried treasures appear. I deeply ponder high and low tides as I walk and conclude that both offer different gifts. High tide is an abundant giver as the shoreline becomes covered with the aqueous surf. The beach is infused with endless, energetic waves of water. Low tide is also a great provider because of what it takes away. As the water recedes, wonderful shapes and colors of glistening sea shells remain on the hard, damp sand. I have always been enchanted by the natural rhythm of the tides.

In life, too, we experience high and low tides. Just like the sea, it is natural for our lives to ebb and flow, and just like the seasons, our lives change and adapt. Things will not always be difficult nor will they always be easy. We cycle to our own rhythm by our openness and the depth of our connection to nature. I think our ability to grow is measured by how we handle our own tides and seasons.

We all experience high tides in our lives when we are replenished by caring people, uplifting experiences or by spending quiet time in nature. Filling our internal shoreline is a priority for those who want to give their best and utmost to others. Often in high tide, we easily move forward and effortlessly walk our path, just as in spring and summer when we are energized by bright sunshine and warmer days.

Low tide, however, offers us something different. When challenges arise, we are unsure of our next steps and nothing seems clear. We need to look deep inside, during the low tide on our uncertain shoreline, to discover the clarity. We need low tide to go within, just like we need the beauty of autumn and the quiet of winter for restoration and sustenance.

The important thing to remember is that each tide, each season is temporary and will bring messages and lessons we need to sustain us on our journey. Having faith in the process and being present in the moments, allow us to discover our deeper truths that set the stage for expansion and growth.

We must have the willingness to be stewards of our own souls, to allow the cleansing and closure of our past so that rebirth and renewal can enter in. Willing to ride the waves, and inhale the salty air. Willing to embrace the seasons of our lives. And remembering that we don't walk the journey alone. Our friends, our Anam Cara, walk with us.

I spent three December days on Cape Cod with Joan and it was an exhilarating experience for me. Outside the window of my cottage was a gnarly tree, similar to the one that captured the essence of my knotted inner landscape at the retreat on Whidbey. This is an appropriate way to close out this "season on the water" as it started, spending time with Joan and bringing this season of my life full circle. We shared daily meals, walked beaches together, and witnessed an incredible sunset in Provincetown while "chasing the light," as Joan called it. In our time together, we enriched our connection and deepened our bond. Reciprocal and nourishing, our friendship strengthens with each encounter.

Although we have known each other a short time, I feel we share a lifelong journey. We are soul friends. I learn much from Joan by watching her live her life from a place of authenticity. She teaches me to trust in the universe and to live into my life's questions. She renders herself vulnerable by the sharing and unveiling of her truth. Her willingness to accept and honor the unfinished woman she is, allows me to fully accept my own incompleteness. For me, someone who loves to have a plan and have things in order, the realization that I will always be unfinished is freeing. It takes away the burden of having to get it all right. What is yet unlived allows for growth and new treasures to come onto my shoreline. The shifting tides and changing seasons of my life beckon adventure. Perhaps I have become a Tidal Woman, as Joan would say, someone who welcomes the highs and lows, who looks beneath the sand, rides the waves, and stays in the flow of life.

I am now in a new season of my life. When I left Joan's retreat on Whidbey Island, she gave me a moon shell as a parting gift. With its perfect spiral, the moon shell represents an inward, solitary journey. As we walked her beach together on Cape Cod, we found an oyster shell. Sprawling and uneven, this shell symbolizes growth. This year has been a time of transformation for me. Just like the opening quote of this book says, *"You cannot step into the same river twice. Each time is different and so are you."*

As I close this season on the water, I wish you grace through your own tides and seasons. I wish you the courage to flow with your own currents in your own rhythm. I wish you the wisdom to trust your own river as it runs its course and circulates new energy through you. Leave the work of paddling upstream to someone else as you point your vessel downstream and gently "go with the flow." I wish you peace, ancient peace, as you "paddle on" the waters of your life.

What season of your life do you find yourself in? Is this where you want to be?

Is it a season you have chosen or a season that has been thrust upon you? Are you in high tide, low tide or ebb tide?

What small steps can you take today; to change your season or your tide, or enhance the one you are in?

"The seas are the
heart's blood of the earth.
Plucked up and kneaded by
the sun and the moon,
the tides are systole and diastole
of earth's veins."

- Henry Beston

The Outermost House
A Year of Life
on the Great Beach of Cape Cod

About the Author

Photo by Joanne Steichmann

Mary Anne Smrz is an avid kayaker who uses insights gained on the water to enrich her own life and the lives of others. She finds depth and meaning in her life from the solitude of kayaking, hiking with her yellow lab, Bayfield and spending time in the restorative sanctuary of the natural world.

In her vocation, Mary Anne is a Certified Financial Planner® who helps her clients find meaning beyond money by identifying and clarifying their beliefs and values. In this holistic process, she creates sound financial plans to help her clients achieve their goals and dreams.

Photo by Josette Songco

In her avocation as a photojournalist, Mary Anne shares her thoughts and musings while kayaking, taking others on an insightful inner journey. In her own quest for authenticity, she encourages others to find the same. She writes from her home in Wisconsin.

Made in the USA
Middletown, DE
12 April 2021